On the Wing

David Elliott

illustrated by Becca Stadtlander

CANDLEWICK PRESS

First edition 2014

Library of Congress Catalog Card Number 2013953538
ISBN 978-0-7636-5324-8

14 15 16 17 18 19 CCP 10 9 8 7 6 5 4 3 2 1

Printed in Shenzhen, Guangdong, China

This book was typeset in Columbus.
The illustrations were done in gouache.

Candlewick Press
99 Dover Street
Somerville, Massachusetts 02144

visit us at www.candlewick.com

For Holly Meade
D. E.

For Michael
R. S.

The Hummingbird

Backward!
Forward!

Here
then
there!

Always
in a
tizzy!

Got
no
time
to
sit
or
sing!

Too
busy!
Busy!
Busy!

The Caribbean Flamingo

Singular . . .
an ember
waiting
to ignite.

In multitude . . .
a conflagration!
The sky is set
alight!

The Crow

Your cunning and your confidence
are wonderful to see,
but your singing voice, my friend,
is pure caw-caw-phony.

The Oriole and the Woodpecker

Music lovers fast await
the first duet
of summer.
Oriole is vocalist.
Woodpecker is drummer.

The Japanese Crane

What music do they hear
that makes them flutter so?
It's early spring;
the cranes are dancing,
dancing in the snow.

The Great Horned Owl

The rabbit cowers in her hole—
the shrew, the muskrat, and the vole.
Night slips on his velvet cowl,
and in it hides the hungry owl.
Who? Who?
Who? Who?

The Australian Pelican

Oh, good heavens!
Oh, my word!
The biggest bill of any bird.

Ask the fish—he's no slouch!
The biggest bill, the biggest pouch!

Oh, good heavens!
Oh, my word!
What an oddball! What a bird!

The Macaw

Who
spilled
the
paint?

The Wandering Albatross

Shearwaters, petrels,
cormorants, gulls . . .
these are the birds
of the rough southern seas.
How they must envy
the impossible ease
with which you fly

over the schooners
and three-masted whalers,
guiding the untethered
souls of lost sailors
home through the winds
of the measureless sky.

The Cardinal

He's a hotshot
valentine.
She's a Plain Jane.
But one without
the other . . .
a song with no refrain.

The Andean Condor

You watched the ancient empires
    come, then go.
How and why they vanished—
    a secret that you know.
Is it your knowledge of this mystery
    that we fear?
Or that one day we, too,
    might disappear?

The Puffin

is unique—
especially
its beak.

The Bowerbird

No fancy feathers
to attract a mate,
first he builds
then decorates
his bower.
How carefully
he constructs
the walls!
(The halls
he fills
with flowers.)

And how anxiously
he arranges
the bright tokens
he collects!
Oh pity then
the bowerbird!
Nature's fussy,
lovesick architect.

The Blue Jay

Your reputation isn't good
in our suburban neighborhood.
So when you're dining at the feeder,
take this advice: Please!
Be sweeter!

The Sparrow

chips from the branch
but wants to roar—
small cousin of tyrannosaur.

The Bald Eagle

We say he is a symbol;
he's a real and living bird.
We say he is majestic;
he does not know this word.
Nor has he heard
of *bird of prey*
though he circles like a prayer

on the rising columns
of the shining,
sun-warmed air.